FRANCISCO
CORONADO

FRANCISCO
CORONADO

Malcolm C. Jensen

A Visual Biography
Illustrated with prints, maps, and photographs

Franklin Watts, Inc. / New York / 1974

For the grandfathers

Historical consultant,
Professor Richard Whittemore
Teachers College, Columbia University

Original maps and drawings by William K. Plummer
Photo research by Selma Hamdan

Frontispiece: The coat of arms of
the Vásquez de Coronado family.

Library of Congress Cataloging in Publication Data

Jensen, Malcolm C
    Francisco Coronado.

  (A Visual biography) *1546 2583*
  SUMMARY: A biography of the Spanish explorer
who in two years traveled over four thousand miles
through the Southwest and Great Plains yet failed
to find what he was searching for.
    1. Vázquez de Coronado, Francisco, 1510–1549
— Juvenile literature. [1. Coronado, Francisco Vásquez de, 1510–1554. 2. Explorers, Spanish] I. Title.
E125.V3J46   979.1′01′0924 [B] [92]
ISBN 0-531-00973-4   73-12087

A Note on the Illustrations

Many of the illustrations in this book were drawn about the time of Coronado's trip of exploration into the Southwest. These prints from the period reveal the Europeans' conception of the New World. Since the Indians' way of living changed very little, the photographs in this book, taken in the late 1800s, probably show the Indians and their pueblos very much as Coronado saw them.

The original maps and drawings done by William K. Plummer are indicated by the initials WKP.

Illustration credits

Library of Congress: pp. vi, 5, 10, 40A, 50B, 54

New York Public Library, Rare Map Collection: p. 6

Museum of Primitive Art: p. 9B

American Museum of Natural History: pp. 9A, 22

Hispanic Society of America: p. 13

Mexican National Tourist Council: p. 17

Smithsonian Institution, National Anthropological Archives, Bureau of American Ethnology Collection: pp. 27, 31, 34, 35, 40B, 46

Museum of the American Indian: p. 28

Kansas State Historical Society: p. 50A

AMERICÆ
PARS QVINTA.

Nobilis & admiratione plena
Hieronymi Benzoni Mediolanensis,
secundæ sectionis Hispanorum, tùm in
Nigrittas seruos suos, tùm in Indos crudelita-
tem, Gallorumq̃ piratarũ de Hispanis toties
reportata spolia; Aduentũ item Hispanorũ
in Nouam Indiæ continentis Hispaniam,
eorumq̃ contra incolas eius regionis
sæuitiam explicans.
Addita ad singula fere Capita scholia, in quibus
res Indiæ luculenter exponuntur.
Accessit præterea Tabula Chorographica Nouæ
Hispaniæ in India Occidentali.

AD
Inuictis RVDOLPH. II. ROM. IMP. AVG.
Omniũ elegantibus figuris in aes incisis expressa à
Theodoro de Bry Leod. ciue Franc. A°. cꓷ Iɔ XCV.

THE KNIGHT IN GOLDEN ARMOR

History is the record of what men have done in their time. The record of history speaks only briefly about Francisco Vásquez de Coronado, but what this Spanish gentleman did was important. Coronado explored what are now the states of Arizona, New Mexico, and Texas, and he lived for a short while on the tall-grass plains of Kansas. He did all of this nearly seventy years before Englishmen started their first permanent settlement in Jamestown, Virginia.

All we know about Coronado comes from a few official documents, a few letters, and a few diaries and memoirs written by men he led for two years through the American Southwest. From these few scraps, historians have figured out how and when Coronado's adventure began, what happened along the way, and how it all ended. But nobody really knows what kind of a man Coronado was — what he thought and felt and believed. When we know the facts about his adventure, we can draw our own conclusions about what kind of man he was.

Francisco Vásquez de Coronado was young, rich, and handsome when he appeared on the stage of history. Unlike many other explorers and conquerors of his time, his actions were neither cruel nor greedy. He was of noble birth, he was an excellent soldier and

The title page of Theodore de Bry's America,
a description of the conquest of the New World.

1

leader of men, and he was a bold and skillful horseman. But Coronado's story is not a happy one.

At first, fate gave Coronado everything: a privileged birth in a world where privilege was of great importance; a good education; an exciting new life in a fabulous New World; wealthy and powerful friends; a wife who was beautiful, rich, and kind. Then fate made him the governor of a huge part of what is now Mexico and promised even more. It put him, a handsome young knight in golden armor, at the head of the largest, most expensive, and best-equipped exploring army ever to be assembled in the New World. And then it sent this army and its noble young leader to look for something that wasn't there.

SPAIN IN THE NEW WORLD

Mexico City, 1538. A grand banquet. The great hallways of the viceroy's palace have been turned into flowering gardens. Lining the hallways are trees bearing fruit ripe for picking. Birds hover and chirp in the trees. A large indoor fountain has been built. A chained jaguar paces in front of it.

Tables are set for five hundred guests. At the main table there are two places of honor. The first is occupied by Viceroy Antonio de Mendoza, ruler of the vast Mexican lands then called New Spain. At the other sits Hernando Cortes, conqueror of Mexico. Seated next to Viceroy Mendoza is a handsome, charming young caballero, Francisco Vásquez de Coronado.

The light of a thousand candles dances upon the plates, the knives, the goblets — all are of gold or silver. This banquet, which began at sunset, will go on for seven hours. Throughout the night, musicians play and singers sing.

The following items are a part of the menu: three salads, each of a different shape and texture; goat and veal prepared in the Genoese manner; pies stuffed with doves and quail; fine white wines; boiled mutton; geese and other fowl, boiled whole with gilded beaks and claws; heads of boars and deer; fruits of every kind; olives; radishes; cheeses; sweets and candies of all descriptions; a spicy drink made with honey; cold cocoa; a sweetened wine drink perfumed with cinnamon and other precious spices.

High-ranking ladies are from time to time presented with great cakes containing live rabbits and birds. When the cakes are opened, the rabbits scamper across the tables and the birds soar away, causing much laughter and pleasure among the guests.

Just eighteen years before, in 1520, on the site of Mexico City stood Tenochtitlán, the capital city of the Aztec Indian empire. From this capital the emperor Montezuma II ruled over five million people. Great temple pyramids rose above the city, temples that gave off an unbelievable stench — from dried blood and severed heads from the countless thousands of human sacrifices of a hundred years. Eighteen years later the magnificent ancient city was gone, the temples had been pulled down and the Spanish viceroy, Antonio de Mendoza, was giving a banquet whose regal extravagance few European monarchs could have matched.

How had this change come about?

In a sense, it had all started in 1492. In that year the Spanish King Ferdinand and Queen Isabella finally drove the Moors out of the province of Granada and thereafter ruled over the whole of Spain for the first time. In 1492 the queen and king also sent the Italian map-maker Christopher Columbus to find a westward all-water route to China and Japan. Instead, Columbus found the Caribbean islands of San Salvador in the Bahamas, Hispaniola, and Cuba. (Hispaniola is the large island now divided between the Dominican Republic and Haiti.)

The Spanish conquest of the New World was the quickest and biggest the world had ever seen. In less than fifty years after Columbus's discovery, Spain took over more land and riches than the ancient Romans had been able to obtain in five hundred years. Soon much of the gold, silver, and jewels from the New World began to pour into the Spanish treasury. Outnumbered a thousand to one, Spanish explorers and conquistadores ("conquerors") toppled three great Indian empires — those of the Aztecs in Mexico, the Incas in Peru, and the Chibchas in Columbia.

The great temple of the Aztecs
in Mexico City, as shown in an
engraving made in the late 1600s.

In conquering the New World, Spanish explorers and the priests who accompanied them destroyed entire civilizations and wiped out whole Indian tribes. But this great time of discovery and military conquest was not only a time of killing and taking and ruining. It was also a time of building and sharing.

Today, in almost half of the western hemisphere the national background of many of the people is Spanish. Spanish is the language in which they speak to each other. The churches they worship in are Catholic churches. In many parts of the western hemisphere there are horses, sheep, cattle, pigs, wheat, rye, oranges, lemons, and sugar cane because the Spanish brought them. Potatoes, corn, and tobacco are grown in Europe and elsewhere because the Spanish took these American Indian plants back to the Old World. In much of the American Southwest, and also in Florida and California, the names of rivers, mountains, and towns are often Spanish names, and the buildings often have a Spanish style. All this did not come about because the Spanish cared *only* about getting gold.

But at first, gold was the most important thing. Columbus had found some in Puerto Rico, Hispaniola, Jamaica, and Cuba; the men who came after him slaughtered and tortured many thousands of Indians trying to get more of it. But by 1521 Hernando Cortes had conquered Mexico City. Soon gold was coming into Spain by the shipload, pure gold in the form of solid bars or gold dust. By 1532, Francisco Pizarro had hacked his way through South America to Peru and the Incas. Pizarro found even more wealth — rooms filled to the ceiling with gold, silver, and precious jewels.

In the end the New World gold and silver helped to ruin Spain by giving it the opportunity to pursue war for almost forty

The Spanish empire in America: called, after 1542, the Viceroyalty of Peru. A map drawn by Gilles Boileau de Bouillon in 1555.

years. This policy exhausted the country's wealth and added to the inflation that was already a problem. But none of the important guests at that glittering feast in Mexico City in 1538 would live to see the decline of Spanish power. During the time Cortes, Mendoza, and Coronado were alive, the Spanish Empire was strong. It was the richest, most powerful empire in the western world.

No one knows what Cortes or Mendoza or Coronado said and thought that evening in 1538, as they sat at the great table, choosing with their fingers — forks and spoons were not in general use then — from an endless array of delicacies. But their thoughts must have turned occasionally to important matters.

Mendoza and Cortes were engaged in a deadly power struggle. The stakes were high: political control of Mexico; the prestige and authority of the Spanish king, of whom Mendoza was the personal representative; and the ownership and control of whatever lands and riches lay to the unknown north.

As far as the king of Spain was concerned, by 1535 the age of the conquistadores was over. The conquistadores had been hard, greedy, and often violent men. Furthermore, many of them came from the lower classes. The Spanish government did not trust its conquistadores. They were a special type — men who might want to become kings themselves in the lands they had conquered.

The conquistadores had carved out a new empire for the king of Spain. But now the time had come to make this empire work — to have colonists, mines, churches, farms, schools, and law courts in what had once been a place to have marvelous adventures. Now the king wanted men in the New World he could trust to follow orders, officials who would be loyal and make sure that the king

Above, an ancient carved jade axe
of the Olmec culture in Mexico.
Below, a gold pendant made in
Panama sometime before 1500.

8

*The cruel methods used by the Spanish
to force the Indains to labor, shown in an
engraving by Theodore de Bry in 1593.*

wasn't cheated out of his share (a fifth) of the gold and silver being mined.

Cortes was a conquistador, one of the greatest. Old, scarred, partly crippled from wounds, popular with the colonists, and still vastly tough and ambitious, Cortes was fighting a losing battle for the control of Mexico. The king had given him a title, marquis of the Valley of Oaxaca, and a huge estate, but had carefully not let him have any official duties or power. But Cortes was turning his vision northward. Perhaps another Mexico was there for the taking. Already he had explored parts of lower California and found a tribe of giant Indians and some pearls. He had outfitted ships that had sailed to the Philippines. In 1539 one of his captains would sail into the Gulf of California, discover the mouth of the Colorado River, and claim everything in sight for the marquis of Oaxaca, not the king of Spain.

Mendoza was in Mexico to put a stop to all this, to clip the old warrior's wings once and for all. Mendoza had other duties besides stopping Cortes, of course. He was supposed to make sure that the laws and policies of the Spanish government were obeyed. He was also supposed to remove from office Nuño de Guzmán, governor of a large area of northern Mexico called New Galicia. Guzmán, a man whose strength of personality and ambition rivaled those of Cortes, was creating a scandal by his cruelty to the Indians. He was also trying to beat Cortes to whatever the north had to offer. Guzmán must go, too.

Mendoza was supposed to make sure that the Indians were fairly treated, not turned into slaves, or worked to death in the gold and silver mines. The king and Church did not want Indians mistreated; they wanted Indians to become citizens — although lowly ones — of the Spanish Empire and members of the Catholic Church. Mendoza was supposed to make sure, for example, that if a Spanish soldier or settler wanted to live with an Indian woman, he married her in church. Mendoza tried to do all these things, and he succeeded in many of them.

In 1538 Mexico no longer had to be explored or conquered — it had to be governed. It was still a frontier area, a place for pioneers; it was still dangerous to live in the small towns or on the big isolated plantations. Soldiers still had to put down Indian uprisings and protect settlers. But it was now also a place for government officials, lawyers, accountants, educated men. Even though he was expected to lead soldiers in battle when necessary, Antonio de Mendoza was not an explorer or conquistador. Neither was the young man he had brought with him to Mexico in 1535 — Francisco Vásquez de Coronado.

THE LURE OF THE SEVEN CITIES

Coronado was born in 1510, in the university town of Salamanca, in the province of León, Spain. His family was old, noble, but not particularly rich. When Coronado's father managed, through a couple of prosperous marriages, to put together a sizeable fortune, he created a *mayorazgo* or family estate. This estate, consisting of the family lands, castle, and other property, at the father's death, had by law to go to the oldest son. This settlement meant that the other children received a noble name, an aristocratic upbringing,

The Spanish port of Cádiz in an engraving of the 1500s.
Along with the city of Seville, 62 miles away, Cádiz
was a center of trade with the American colonies.

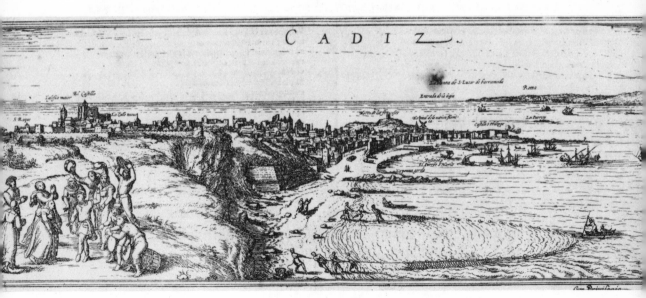

and a small amount of money. And that was all. Younger sons had to earn their own fortunes and obtain their own lands. Coronado was a younger son.

In 1535 Mendoza included Coronado in the large group of aides he brought with him to Mexico City. One writer — but only one — says that Mendoza was Coronado's uncle. No one is sure about that, but it is clear that Mendoza liked and trusted Coronado.

Coronado was just one of many noble younger sons in Mexico. Yet he rose very quickly there. In 1536, he married Beatríz de Estrada, the daughter of the immensely rich royal treasurer of Spain. Beatríz was well known not only for her beauty but also for her kindness and public spirit. She was often spoken of as "Beatríz the Saint." She and her husband started the first charitable organization in the New World — a home for orphaned girls. Beatríz' mother was so pleased with Coronado that she gave him half of a very rich estate called Tlapa.

Mendoza advanced Coronado rapidly. He sent Coronado to put down a rebellion of black slaves and Indians at a silver mine. Coronado managed the assignment efficiently, with a minimum of killing. Mendoza then appointed Coronado a *regidor*, or city councilman, of Mexico City. He also made Coronado his *maestresala*, a sort of personal right-hand man, advisor, and social secretary. In August of 1538 he appointed Coronado, then twenty-eight years old, governor of New Galicia in place of Nuño de Guzmán. Mendoza had arrested Guzmán, put him in prison, and then sent him back to Spain. Guzmán spent years fighting red tape in the Spanish courts and then died, ignored and poverty-stricken, as did many of the early conquistadores.

Coronado's speedy rise in Mexico was not undeserved; he was young, popular, and well connected through his marriage; he had handled the tasks given him up to then with competence. But it is also likely that Mendoza saw in Coronado a useful chess piece — a knight, perhaps — with which to checkmate Cortes. Apart from his other good qualities, Coronado had several outstanding attributes as far as Mendoza was concerned. Unlike Cortes, he was loyal to Mendoza. Unlike Cortes, Coronado could not claim that any part of the New World was legally his to explore, conquer, and own.

By 1538 the Spanish believed that the land to the north of Mexico promised to contain the richest prize in all the New World — the Seven Cities of the Seven Bishops. For centuries Europeans had talked about the story of seven rich bishops, driven out of Portugal by the Moors in the eighth century. These bishops, it was said, had crossed a great body of water and landed in another world called Antilia; here they had built seven great cities, possibly of gold. Most educated Europeans believed this story, just as they believed the legend of the lost continent of Atlantis. The fact that the story told of seven bishops and seven cities made it even more believable, because seven has always been a number with special meaning, throughout man's history.

The story of the Seven Cities was a legend. Legend is a kind of memory, a story that comes down from the past. Like all memory, legend sometimes confuses things or remembers only part of what happened. But the amazing thing is that, in one way or another, many legends have turned out to be true. For thousands of years, people thought the account of Helen and the city of Troy was just a Greek story that poets liked to tell and retell. Then in the 1870s, a man who *believed* this legend went out and dug up the ruins of Troy.

In the sixteenth century the New World was a strange, magical place. It contained many, many mysteries. There were kings so rich they made toys out of pure gold. Cities made of huge stone blocks stood on high mountaintops — even today we aren't sure how men built such cities. Twenty-ton human heads, carved out of stone, lay in thick jungles that a man could scarcely move in. There were great discs, the size of wagon wheels, made of pure silver; some of these discs were engraved or carved with calendars more accurate than any Europeans knew of. In fact, these calendars were more accurate than the one we use today.

There were also Indian priests who cut the hearts out of living men. There were kings whose favorite food was the roasted flesh of young boys. There were wonderful new medicines and horrible new poisons. There were fabulous new animals, even birds that talked. There were new foods. There was even a plant people could smoke. All these things were *real*. And since the New World was a place in which many marvelous and unbelievable things had been found, many people were certain that the Seven Cities would sooner or later be discovered there.

Viceroy Mendoza was a brilliant politician. But he was also a very sensible, cautious man. There had been many reports and rumors, most of them from Indians, about seven rich cities to the north. Mendoza studied all these reports. One of the most intriguing came from three Spanish gentlemen and one black slave who had made an incredible journey.

These four men, shipwrecked survivors of a Spanish expedition, had struggled through the Florida Everglades. They had paddled in rafts to what is now Galveston, Texas. And from there they had walked, more than a thousand miles, to Mexico. They had lived among the Indians for almost six years, sometimes treated as slaves, sometimes as godlike medicine men.

In 1536, these four men — Cabeza de Vaca, Alonso del Castillo, Andres Dorantes, and Estéban, who belonged to Dorantes — were questioned closely by Mendoza. Each reported that the Indians had confirmed the story of seven immensely rich cities called Cíbola. These cities were to be found somewhere in what is now New Mexico, across a great *despoblado* or desert. The re-

A large ancient stone sculpture
of the Olmec culture in Mexico.

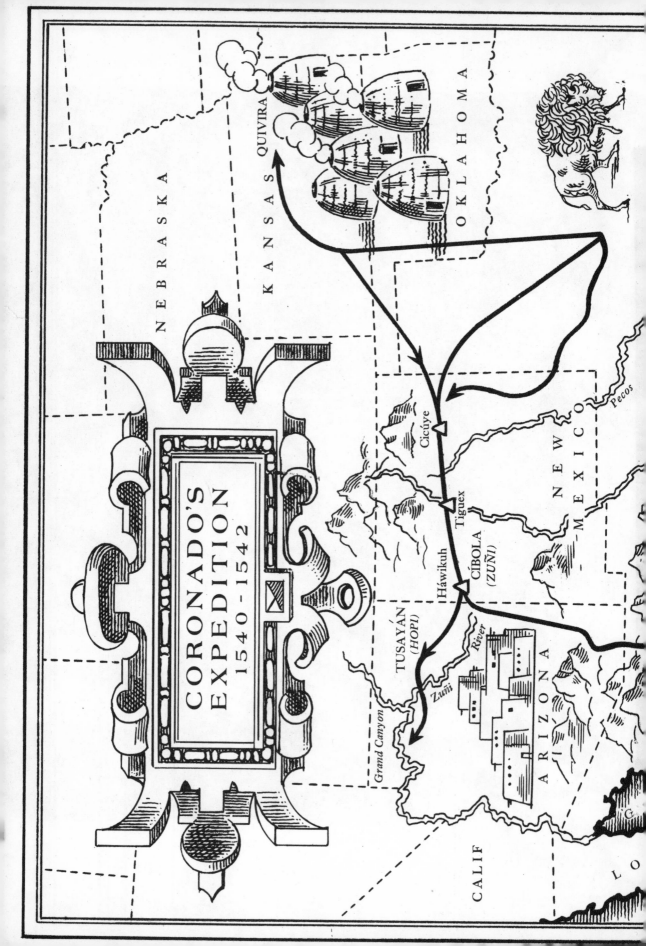

CORONADO'S EXPEDITION 1540 - 1542

NEBRASKA

KANSAS

QUIVIRA

OKLAHOMA

NEW MEXICO

Pecos

Cicuye

Tiguex

CÍBOLA (ZUÑI)

Háwikuh

TUSAYÁN (HOPI)

Grand Canyon

Zuñi River

ARIZONA

CALIF

LO

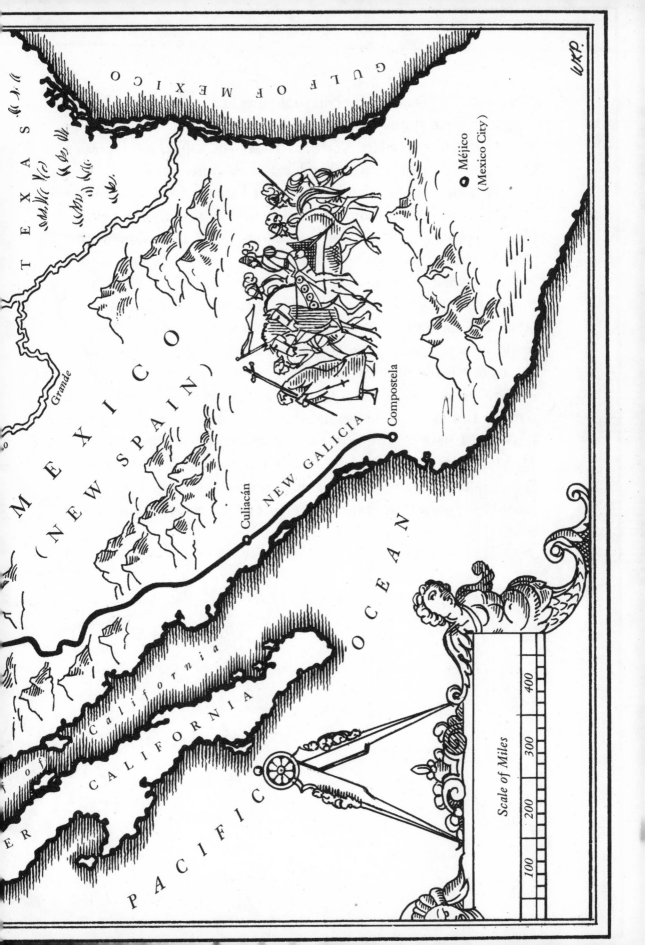

GULF OF MEXICO

TEXAS

Rio Grande

MEXICO

(NEW SPAIN)

Méjico
(Mexico City)

Compostela

Culiacán

NEW GALICIA

PACIFIC OCEAN

Gulf of California

CALIFORNIA

LOWER California

WKP.

Scale of Miles

100   200   300   400

ports from De Vaca and his companions tallied with many others. Together these rumors added up to a pattern, exactly the same sort of pattern that had led Cortes to the Aztecs' capital and Pizzaro to the land of the Incas. Another Mexico! Another Peru!

Mendoza laid his plans. He bought Estéban from Dorantes. Estéban knew part of the route, had a good idea where the Seven Cities were to be found, and was accomplished in dealing with Indians. He had even obtained a special rattle, an object that many Indians seemed to view with respect and awe. Mendoza decided to send out a scouting party guided by Estéban. Then he sent another scouting party to confirm the results of the first one. Meanwhile, he began the expensive and time-consuming task of preparing a great exploring expedition that would be able not only to explore but also to conquer. He let it be known that he was considering Coronado as the leader of this expedition. Upon hearing this news, Cortes sailed for Spain to complain to the king, leaving Mendoza a free hand. Mendoza was a political genius. But had he been less than a genius, had he done his job less well, Coronado would have ended his days as an important, respected, and happy man.

WITH SILVER WINE GOBLETS

Compostela, capital of New Galicia, Mexico. February 23, 1540. Two dozen smallish buildings, some of them stone or adobe, others makeshift affairs of wood and skins. Swirling around these buildings, a great noisy mass of men and animals. A thousand cattle, goats, and sheep. Almost a thousand horses and mules, many of them laden with pots, pans, blankets, cups, knives, and other camping gear. Some carry beads, mirrors, and other cheap, shiny goods — these will be used as gifts for the Indians. Some carry silver candlesticks, silver wine goblets, fine lace tablecloths — these will be used by the young noblemen while they are on the trail. Six or seven hundred Indians and blacks, mostly men but some women and children — they will manage the animals and take care of other tasks. About sixty foot soldiers, mostly Spanish, but a few Portuguese, a few Italians, and one Scotsman. Some wear swords or daggers; some carry crossbows or harquebuses — huge, heavy rifles that must be propped up by tripods to aim them. Most of these infantrymen wear thick leather coats as armor; some carry leather shields; most of these soldiers are small, slender men, about five and half feet tall. There are over two hundred horsemen, most of them gentlemen. These men are also small; some wear metal armor, but many wear buckskin. Most of them are very young — in their late teens or early twenties. Some carry swords and lances, but many carry heavy clubs, great flat wooden things like swords, with pieces of sharp stone set in the edges. There are also four friars, quiet men in brown robes and leather sandals.

Coronado starting on his search for the Seven Cities. A painting done by Frederic Remington in 1905.

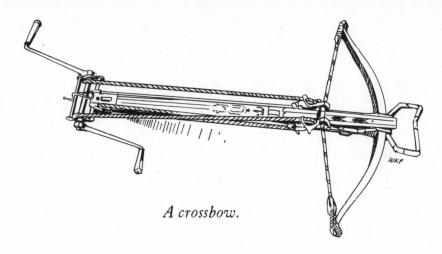

A crossbow.

Bugles blow, flags wave, animals scream, men shout, dust rises — and this enormous mass moves slowly northward. In front of this crowd rides a young man on a large, nervous horse. The young man's armor is gold-plated, and it blazes like a small sun. Thus Francisco Vásquez de Coronado led his army to the Seven Cities — and beyond.

This army had cost Viceroy Mendoza 60,000 ducats to equip and send out. Coronado had put in another 50,000 ducats, mostly borrowed — in today's money, about a million dollars.

The four friars walked just behind Coronado. They walked quickly, easily. Two of them had walked across South America and back — over mountains, through swamps and jungles. One of them, Fray Marcos de Niza, a Frenchman, had seen the Seven Cities of Cíbola from a distance. It was his *relación* or report that was directly responsible for this expedition.

When, in 1536, the rumors about the Seven Cities had started coming in, the Bishop of Mexico had told Viceroy Mendoza to send priests instead of soldiers, so that "the conquest may be Christian and not a butchery." Mendoza sent Fray Marcos, guided by Estéban. They left northern Mexico on March 7, 1539. Estéban and some Indian companions went ahead and traveled fast. They sent back to Fray Marcos, who was about a day behind, huge wooden crosses, which meant that everything was going well and that the Seven Cities were fabulously rich. Just before he got to the Seven Cities of Cíbola, Fray Marcos was met by some of Estéban's Indian companions. Estéban had been killed at the Seven Cities.

He had been killed because the rattle he carried meant something very bad to the people of Cíbola. And Estéban also asked for turquoises and women. The Cíbolans thought Estéban was a bad man and would lead other bad men to their city. So they killed him.

Fray Marcos bravely decided to take a look at Cíbola anyway. He looked at it from a distance of about a mile, and then he walked quickly back to Compostela — a distance of almost one thousand miles!

The report that Fray Marcos made in Mexico City on September 2, 1539, was full of errors. But Fray Marcos did not say that Cíbola was rich and full of gold. He reported what Indians told him about an *abra* or valley where people had gold dishes and pots and even had little gold knives to scrape off their sweat. This *abra* was about three-quarters of the way to Cíbola. Cíbola itself, Marcos said, was a pueblo — an Indian town — at the base of a hill. This pueblo was larger than Mexico City. And that was all Fray Marcos said.

But Fray Marcos's report was talked about in all Mexico, especially in the churches, which were the main source of news. After a while, people said that Fray Marcos had seen this: "White people. They wear clothes and sleep in beds. They have many emeralds and other jewels but they don't care about these. They like turquoises better. They have cotton, but like animal skins better. They use pots and pans of gold, because they have no other metals. There is much gold there, more than in Peru. And there are seven cities, just like this one."

Early in 1540, Viceroy Mendoza sent another scouting party to make sure of the report. The party was made up of a few men led by Melchior Díaz, a fine and honest soldier. Díaz got the true story, but he didn't get back before Coronado had left Compostela.

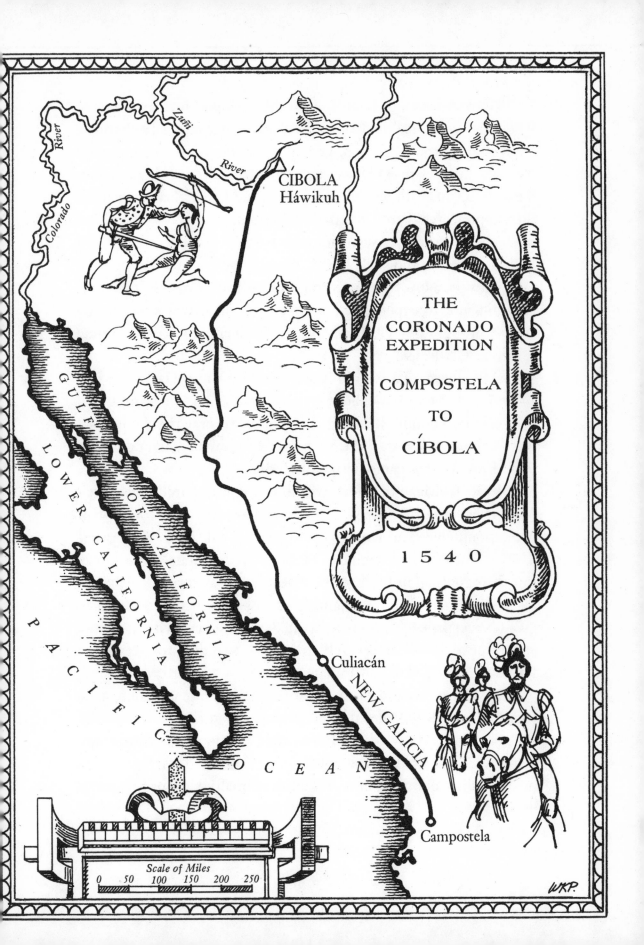

THE
CORONADO
EXPEDITION

COMPOSTELA

TO

CÍBOLA

1 5 4 0

CÍBOLA
Háwikuh

Zuñi

River

Colorado River

GULF OF CALIFORNIA

LOWER CALIFORNIA

PACIFIC OCEAN

Culiacán

NEW GALICIA

Campostela

Scale of Miles
0   50   100   150   200   250

WKP.

Coronado set out from Compostela leading the march north. About halfway between Compostela and Culiacán, the last Spanish outpost in northern Mexico, he met Melchoir Díaz returning and received his report. Díaz's report to Coronado was kept secret. That didn't help, though, since everybody knew that *good* news isn't kept secret. From then on, Coronado had to deal with an army that was uneasy, suspicious, and touchy.

Between Compostela and Culiacán, there was a minor skirmish between a few Spaniards and Indians. But Coronado's second-in-command, an experienced and valuable man, was killed by an arrow through the eye. In his place, Coronado appointed García López de Cárdenas.

At Culiacán, Coronado wisely decided to proceed with just a fraction of his army — about eighty cavalrymen, thirty infantry, and some two hundred Indians. It is with this force that he pressed on to Cíbola. The rest of the army could follow behind at a slower pace. Fray Marcos came with Coronado.

From Culiacán to Cíbola was about eight hundred miles. Fray Marcos had said that the way was easy. Actually, the route went over mountains that wore out the hooves of sheep and goats. They had to be left behind. On slippery mountain cliffs horses lost their footing and fell to their death. It was spring, so the Indians they met were just planting crops; they had little food to give. Nevertheless, Coronado treated the Indians with courtesy and respect. He once severely punished a soldier for stealing a few ears of corn from an Indian.

As Coronado and his men moved north, into Arizona, they found a few river valleys where there was grass for the horses. But not often. Many of the horses died. Some of the Indian servants were not used to the cold, and several died. A few of the men ate a poisonous plant and died. But finally Coronado and his

*A pueblo near Cíbola in New Mexico,
as it appeared in 1879.*

The Zuñi pueblo, probably the same pueblo that was known as Cíbola.

men reached the Zuñi River, just where it flows from New Mexico into Arizona. And there was Cíbola.

It was an Indian pueblo, a sort of town made of adobe apartment houses "all crumpled together," looking to the Spaniards like houses in the poor part of cities in their own country.

Coronado approached the Cíbolans waiting in front of their town. He read them a long speech telling them that they were good people but now they belonged to the king of Spain, a great white chief across the sea.

The Cíbolans attacked.

Most of the Cíbolans — today we would call them Zuñi Indians — were inside their homes, waiting to shoot down at the Spaniards. Several times Coronado tried to speak with Cíbolans outside, but each time they shot arrows. Finally even Fray Marcos became angry. "Take your shields and go after them!" he shouted.

Coronado gave the signal to attack Cíbola. Most of the Indians were protected in the buildings. The soldiers had to climb ladders in their heavy armor to get at the warriors. Coronado's men were tired from their long march, so tired they couldn't work their crossbows and harquebuses. But they were also famished. All they had eaten for the last month was a little corn bread. There was food in Cíbola.

And so they charged into deadly battle, these fine young men of Spain. They were attacking not for gold, or glory, or honor. They were rushing into the fight for some corn and beans and turkey and a little salt.

Coronado led his men into the thick of the action. A great plume waved from his helmet. His golden armor glittered. His deadly Toledo sword flashed coldly in the sun. The Zuñi, being a sensible people, did a sensible thing. They looked down at the golden knight and dropped rocks on his head, knocking him unconscious.

"I WISH I HAD BETTER NEWS..."

When Coronado woke up, Cíbola had been captured. His life had been saved by García López de Cárdenas and another young knight — Hernando de Alvarado.

The Zuñi had surrendered after an hour's fighting. They asked to leave Cíbola and were allowed to go. Then the soldiers sat down for what was to them a heavenly feast.

Cíbola was actually a pueblo called Háwikuh. Coronado and others said there were seven such cities, in a fifteen-mile radius, with Cíbola being the name for all seven. But archaeologists have found the ruins of only six.

Coronado and his small army reached Háwikuh on July 7, 1540. For the next several months they lived there. Eventually many of the people of Háwikuh moved back into their homes, although they kept most of the women hidden away. The Spaniards and the Zuñi actually got along fairly well together.

On August 3, 1540, Coronado sent a messenger back to Mexico City with a long letter for Viceroy Mendoza. In this letter, Coronado explained what had happened so far, and that there were no riches at Cíbola. The whole expedition was a failure.

He described the attack on Háwikuh, and praised his men: "All these gentlemen and soldiers bore themselves well, as was expected of them." A few soldiers were wounded, but no one was killed.

*A scene of a terrace in the
Zuñi pueblo, as it appeared in 1879.*

Then Coronado wrote:

[Fray Marcos] has not told the truth in a single thing that he said . . . except the name of the cities and the large stone houses. For, although they are not decorated with turquoises, nor made of lime and good bricks, nevertheless they are very good houses, three and four and five stories high, where there are very good homes and good rooms with corridors, and some quite good rooms underground. . . . Most of the ladders which they have for their houses are movable and portable and taken up and placed wherever desired. . . .

The people of the towns are fairly large, and intelligent. . . . Most of them are entirely naked except for the covering of their privy parts. They also have painted blankets which they wear. . . . They are well-built and handsome. They have some turquoises I think, but they took them away and hid them. . . . We also found a few tiny emeralds, rather poor. . . .

The food they eat . . . consists of maize, which they have in great abundance, beans, and game which they must eat (although they say they do not) because we have found many skins of deer, hare, and rabbits. They make the best tortillas I have seen anywhere. . . . They have very good salt, in crystals. . . . There are many animals, bears, tigers, lions, porcupines, and some sheep as big as horses. . . .

God knows that I wish I had better news to write to your Lordship.

Coronado also mentioned that among his army "there is not one pound of raisins, nor sugar, nor oil, nor wine, except barely half a quart, which is saved to say Mass." And he told Mendoza that he was continuing the search for gold and silver, sending scouting parties in all directions. He was also sending with the letter some painted skins, a few maps, some blankets, some native weapons, and a few other small items. Coronado didn't say so, but he was also sending back Fray Marcos, who was now extremely unpopular.

One of the exploring parties Coronado sent out was led by Captain Pedro de Tovar. About 160 miles northwest of Háwikuh,

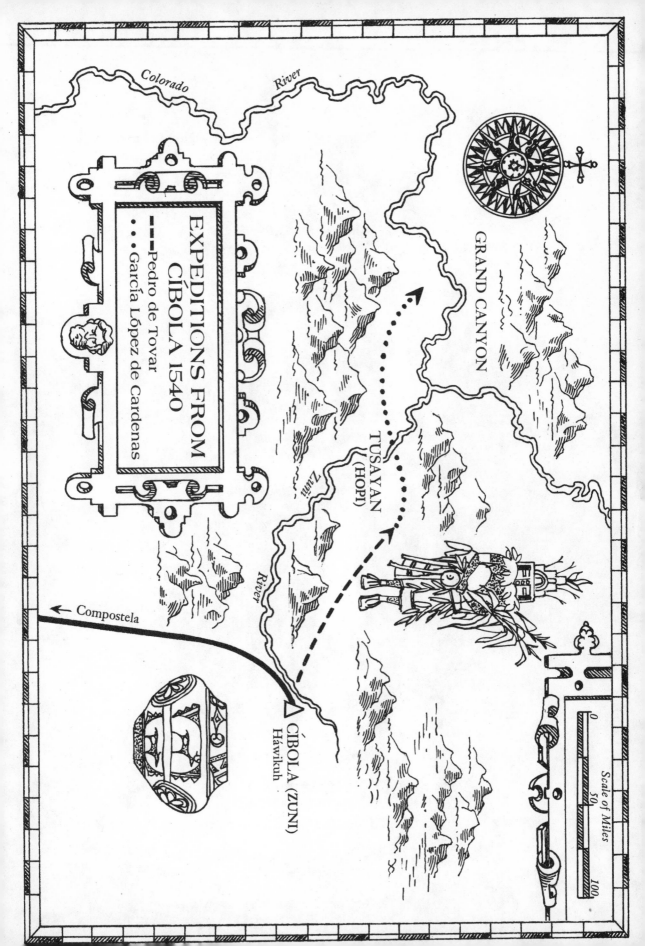

Colorado River

GRAND CANYON

EXPEDITIONS FROM
CÍBOLA 1540

━ ━ ━ Pedro de Tovar
• • • • García López de Cardenas

Zuñi

TUSAYAN
(HOPI)

River

← Compostela

CÍBOLA (ZUNI)
Háwikuh

Scale of Miles

0

50

100

*Left, three young Hopi maidens
wearing their hair in a
traditional style. A photo of 1879.*

*Above, the Hopi snake dance.
A photo of 1897.*

in what is now northern Arizona, Captain Tovar met a very great people, although he did not know it. He found the Hopi Indians, at a place the Spanish called Tusayán. All Tovar saw were Indians who looked just like the Zuñi, living in typical pueblos on top of high mesas.

But the Hopi were an ancient, very wise people — and still are. The Hopi legends and religion — a very complicated, very beautiful one — say that after many wanderings the Hopi settled where Tovar found them, and where Hopi still live today. They *chose* to settle there, because living there is so difficult that men cannot manage it unless they are very strong and very wise, and pay close attention to the ways and powers of nature. If foolish or greedy men try to live in the Hopi's dry, windy land, they will soon starve and die.

The Hopi knew that the white man was coming. They knew that Taiowa, the Creator, had made four races of men: black, red, yellow, and white. That is why the Hopi corn had kernels of those four colors — to remind them of the four races of men, and to remind them that one day the races would come together again and live in peace. Long ago, these races had separated. But one day, Pahana — the lost white brother from across the water — would return. In fact, the ancient legends said he would return in the very same year that Cortes came to Mexico. But he might also be twenty years late, as Tovar was.

The Hopi knew just what to do when the lost white brother came. A Hopi chief would hold out his hand, palm up. Then Pahana would clasp his hand in a special way, making the sign of universal brotherhood. When Captain Tovar came, a Hopi wise man put out his hand in the special way. Tovar dropped a little present in it.

Then the Hopi knew that this was not Pahana. They told Tovar to go away. There was a scuffle. A priest named Juan de Padilla, who had been a soldier in his youth, finally lost his temper. "To tell the truth," he shouted angrily, "I don't know what we

36

came for!" The Spanish battlecry was given: *Santiago y a ellos!* ("Saint James and have at them!") There was a brief fight, and then the Hopi gave up.

The Hopi told Captain Tovar about a great river to the west. Perhaps the captain and his men could learn a little wisdom by looking at it. Tovar went back to Coronado and told him about the river the Hopi had mentioned. Coronado sent García López de Cárdenas to look for it. And so Cárdenas and his group were the first white men to see the Grand Canyon of the Colorado. They tried for three days to climb down into it, but couldn't. Then they came back and reported to Coronado. But Coronado himself never saw the canyon.

While Coronado was staying at Háwikuh, Indians came to him from the east, from a pueblo called Cicúye, near what is now Santa Fe, New Mexico. One of these Indians, an important chief, the Spanish named Bigotes ("Whiskers") because of his mustache. Bigotes said that Coronado would be welcome at Cicúye. He also told Coronado about Tiguex, a comfortable land about 170 miles to the east of Háwikuh. Tiguex was a town of twelve large pueblos, in the Rio Grande valley, about twenty miles north of what is now Albuquerque, New Mexico.

Coronado sent Hernando de Alvarado — who was twenty-three years old — to go with Bigotes and explore. Bigotes led Alvarado and twenty men to Tiguex. There was plenty of food and much green grass for the horses. Alvarado sent a messenger back to Coronado to tell him that Tiguex was an ideal place for the whole army to spend the winter.

Then Alvarado went on eastward to Cicúye, where Bigotes gave him and his men a warm welcome and a great feast. Then Alvarado said he wanted to go farther east. Bigotes sent with him an Indian the Spanish named the Turk, because they thought "he looked like one." The Turk was a slave, having been captured by Bigotes in battle. The Turk's people lived on the Great Plains to

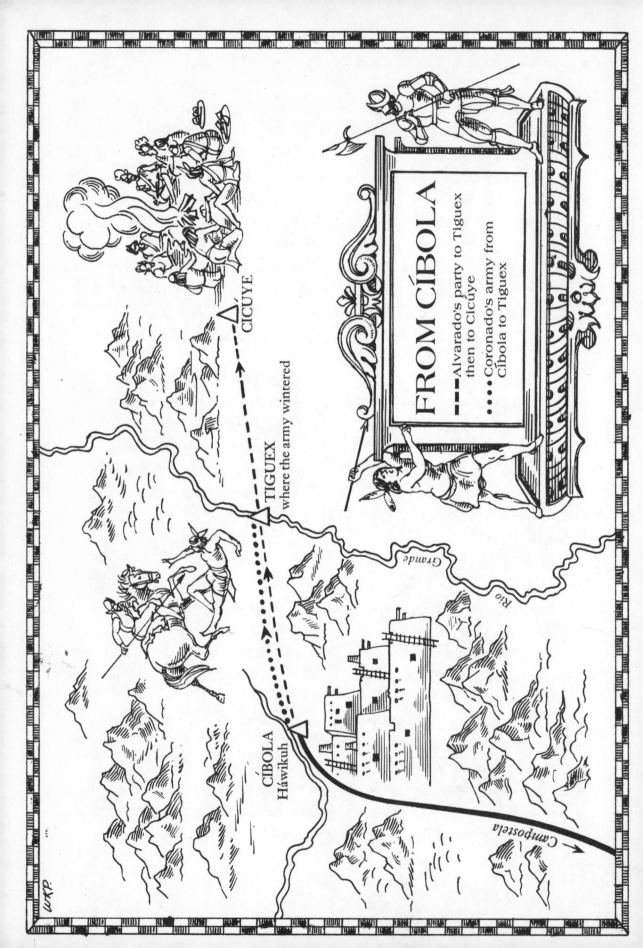

FROM CÍBOLA

■■■ Alvarado's party to Tiguex
      then to Cicúye

•••• Coronado's army from
      Cíbola to Tiguex

CICUYE

TIGUEX
where the army wintered

Rio Grande

CÍBOLA
Háwikuh

Campostela

the northeast — in a country called Quivira. The Turk led Alvarado almost to the Texas border, where they could look out over the plains.

As Alvarado and his men stared at the great ocean of grass and the endless herds of buffalo, the Turk told them something that made them forget about all that. Quivira, he said, was a land with a great river, and the fish in it were as big as horses. There were big boats, with forty oarsmen. Eagles made of gold were fastened to the boats. The great lord of Quivira rested under trees that had little golden bells hanging in them. He, the Turk, could take them there right away. There — and he pointed across the plains to the northeast, toward Kansas.

But Alvarado had to turn back, and he returned to Cicúye. The Turk told Alvarado that he had a gold bracelet from Quivira. Bigotes had taken it from him, he said. When asked about it, Bigotes replied that the Turk was lying — there was no gold bracelet, and there was no gold in Quivira. What a ridiculous story! The people of Quivira lived in grass huts!

Alvarado then did a dangerous and dishonorable thing. He tricked Bigotes and another chief and put them in chains. Then he took them — and the Turk — back to Tiguex.

It was about eighty days since Alvarado left Háwikuh. In the meantime, Coronado had moved his small advance army from Háwikuh to Tiguex. It was now early December, it was extremely cold, and the rest of Coronado's army would arrive shortly.

Although Coronado was strict with his men, and tried to be fair and diplomatic with the Indians at Tiguex, trouble developed. There was not enough warm clothing, and soldiers started taking blankets from the Indians. Coronado asked the people to vacate one of the pueblos, so that his army could live there. One soldier insulted a married Indian woman. The Indians were ready to explode. And then Alvarado got back with Bigotes.

Bigotes was a proud, honest, sensible man — that is why he was a chief. When he denied knowing anything about a gold bracelet, Coronado let soldiers sic dogs on Bigotes, to torture him into telling the truth.

Coronado was not a cruel or hasty man. When he let Bigotes be tortured, he must have been desperate. This was his last chance to find a great kingdom — to find gold. He *had* to know if Bigotes was telling the truth. He knew there would be trouble with the Tiguex Indians if they saw a chief of the Cicúye people being chewed by dogs. But Coronado took the chance — and lost.

The people of Tiguex revolted. They killed some of the horses — many of them belonging to García López de Cárdenas — and tried to kill some of the men who were guarding them.

There were actually two battles in Tiguex, at two different pueblos, at two different times. The first took place in late December, 1540, at a pueblo called Arenal, just one day before the rest of Coronado's army arrived. Coronado ordered the attack on Arenal, but was not actually there. The soldiers were led by Cárdenas, and they did a terrible thing.

Nobody knows exactly how it happened, but a group of Indians surrendered, and a Spaniard decided to tie them to posts and burn them to death. Two hundred posts were set up, but nobody knows how many Indians were burned. It was at least thirty. The Spaniards' intention was to show the other Indians what happened when they tried to kill Spaniards. Cárdenas was later blamed for this act, because he was in command. Cárdenas said he hadn't told anybody to do that — it was just something that happened in the heat of battle. But setting up two hundred posts isn't something

Above, the American buffalo,
as seen in a woodcut done in 1554.

Below, the pueblo of San Ildefonso,
as it appeared in 1879.

that is done in a moment of fury or hate. Somebody *deliberately* burned unarmed Indian prisoners to death. For this act, García López de Cárdenas, the discoverer of the Grand Canyon, later spent seven years as a prisoner in Spain.

Somewhat later, another Tiguex pueblo called Moho rebelled. Many of the warriors from all the Tiguex pueblos went there to take a stand.

If the revolt in Moho was not put down, no Spaniard would be safe in Tiguex. And if Coronado was going to explore to the east, he had to have a secure winter base in Tiguex.

Moho was a very strong pueblo, and Coronado was not able to take it. So he encircled it, allowing no one to escape. Then he blocked a stream that ran through Moho, so the people would run out of water. During the winter months of 1540-1541, the people of Moho held out; they melted snow for water. But in the spring, the water finally ran out. The Indians tried to dig a well, but it collapsed, killing those who were digging it. Finally the warriors sent out the women and children. Then one night the warriors tried to break out. The Spanish caught and killed many of them. Then Coronado burned Moho to the ground.

Most of the people in all the Tiguex pueblos went away and would not come back to their homes, even though Coronado begged them to do so. He had lost their trust and friendship forever.

Perhaps 350 Indians — warriors — were killed in the battles of Arenal and Moho. Six or seven Spaniards were killed. Nothing can excuse what happened in Tiguex. Coronado and his men are stained by what they did, and their great adventure becomes much less than it might have been.

But remember too that the caballeros were alone and outnumbered in a strange new land, and they thought that their lives, their fortunes, and the honor of Spain would be lost if they did not

42

show the people of Tiguex who ruled. Remember too that 350 years later, in South Dakota, at a place called Wounded Knee, men wearing the uniform of the United States Army opened fire on a camp of unarmed Sioux Indians and did not stop until about two hundred men, women, and little children were dead.

GOOD WATER AND PLUM TREES

Tiguex, New Mexico. December 27, 1541, almost exactly one year after the battle of Arenal. It is a cold bright day. The soldiers are bored, restless, quarrelsome. They are covered with lice. They have been cooped up in Tiguex for several months with nothing to do. They are waiting for spring, because they are anxious to explore further the new land they have found to the northeast — Quivira.

A horse race has been arranged to provide some entertainment. Two men, Francisco Coronado and Don Rodrigo Maldonado, will race. At the signal, the horses leap forward and pound across the frozen ground. Coronado is slightly in the lead. Suddenly Coronado's saddle twists loose, and Coronado is pitched to the ground in front of Maldonado. Maldonado tries to jump his horse over the fallen Coronado and almost makes it. But one of the hooves smashes Coronado in the head.

For many days after the accident, Coronado lay in a coma. He did not die, but a part of his brain and personality did. And here too died the great adventure. Coronado thought he was going to die, and he wanted to die in Mexico City, with his wife and children at his side. So he took his entire army back to Mexico and abandoned all that he had found. What he had found was a beautiful new country called Quivira — what is now central Kansas.

In the spring of 1541 Coronado had led his entire army out of Tiguex, toward the east — toward the great rich kingdom the

Turk had described, where golden bells hung from trees. From what the Turk told him, Coronado believed that this kingdom might be a Christian one, since its king, called Tatarrax, read from a sacred book and worshiped a queen of heaven. Perhaps here at last were the ancient Seven Cities of the lost seven bishops!

The army marched east to Cicúye, where Coronado finally let Bigotes go. Then they crossed into Texas and came upon a great plain that the Spanish called *Llano Estacado* — the Staked Plains. They saw the vast herds of buffalo. They met some Plains Apaches who lived in tents and followed the buffalo.

But as they entered Texas, the Turk lied to them again. He led them *south*, farther into Texas, instead of northeast toward Quivira and Kansas. For more than a month, the army wandered southward on plains so flat and broad and empty that if a man wandered away from camp there was not a single landmark to guide him back. There was a severe hailstorm; the hailstones dented armor, and killed some horses.

Finally, another Indian guide named Isopete, who was also from Quivira, refused to go any farther. The Turk was trying to kill them — to wear out the horses and starve the army to death. Why, nobody really knows. It could be that the Turk was just completely evil — or perhaps he had decided the Indians would be better off without the Spaniards around. Finally, Coronado put the Turk in chains and believed Isopete.

Coronado took thirty of his best horsemen and a few foot soldiers and set out northward, guided by Isopete. The rest of the army returned to Tiguex.

In about thirty-five days of marching, Coronado and his companions came to Quivira. Quivira was exactly what Bigotes had said it was — a group of grass huts.

The pueblo of Taos, north of
Tiguex, as it appeared in 1900.

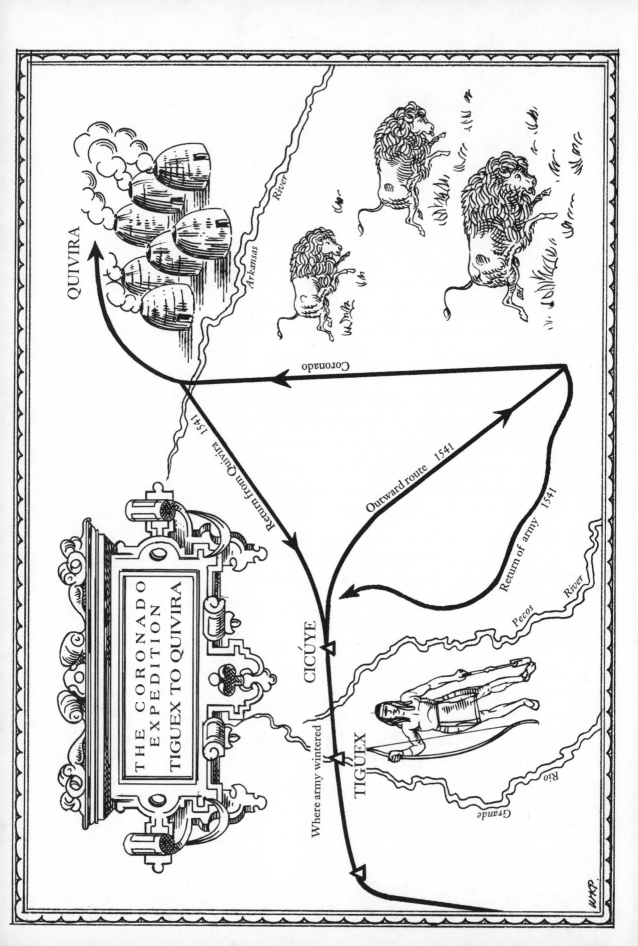

THE CORONADO EXPEDITION TIGUEX TO QUIVIRA

QUIVIRA

Arkansas River

Coronado

Return from Quivira 1541

Outward route 1541

Return of army 1541

Pecos River

CICÚYE

Where army wintered

TIGUEX

Río Grande

W.H.P.

The Quivirans — Wichita Indians — were handsome and huge. The Spanish said they were seven feet tall. Everybody thought they were exaggerating, until recently seven-foot Indian skeletons were dug up in Saline County, Kansas.

Coronado stayed in Quivira for about a month. Then some of his men strangled the Turk, and they all went back to Tiguex.

There was no gold in Quivira. But the real wealth of Quivira did not escape Coronado and his men. They saw it for what it was, one of the richest farmlands in the world. There were good water, plum trees, deep rich topsoil. One of the men who saw it said that it was better land for farming than anything in France, Spain, or Italy.

Most of the men who saw central Kansas were younger sons of noble birth. They had no lands of their own. They had nothing to do in Mexico but make nuisances of themselves — they were unemployed gentlemen. But here *was* something. They could carve out great estates here, bring in farmers and peasants to settle and work the land. They could raise cattle and horses, and live the life of wealthy landowners. This was really what they had come to the New World for.

And so Coronado promised that they would go back to Tiguex, spend the winter there, and then return the following spring to Quivira.

But this never happened. Before the accident, Coronado had been, as one of his men said, "the most beloved and best obeyed leader who had ever ventured forth in the Indies." Afterwards, he became fearful, furtive, and unfair. It was difficult for his friends to like him anymore. He wanted to go back to Mexico. So did many of the soldiers. But many of the officers did not. One priest, Juan de Padilla, decided to go back to Quivira to teach the Indians. Sixty soldiers asked to go with him, to protect him. But Coronado

49

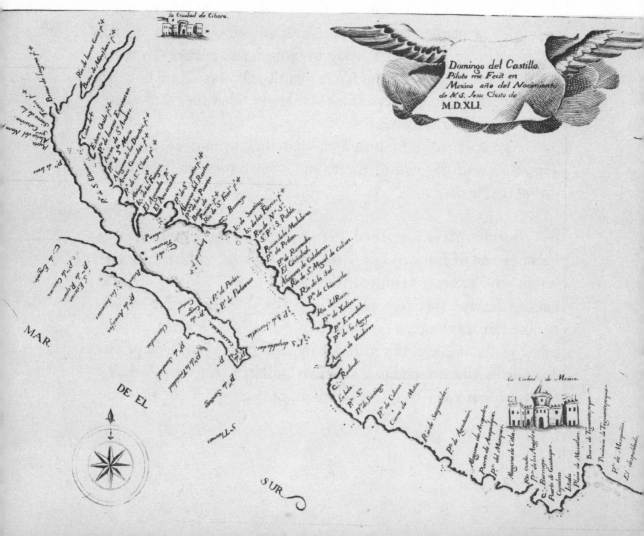

la Ciudad de Cibora.

Domingo del Castillo,
Piloto me Fecit en
Mexico año del Nacimiento
de N.S. Jesu Chisto de
M.D.XLI.

MAR

DE EL

SUR

la Ciudad de Mexico.

said no. So Juan de Padilla went back to Quivira without any soldiers. He lived there a few months and then was killed.

Coronado's officers were gentlemen, and they had given their word to obey him. They did, and they went back to Mexico with him.

And so in early April, 1542, Coronado led his entire army back to Culiacán, Mexico — a distance of some nine hundred miles. Much of the time he was too sick to ride a horse and was carried in a stretcher. But he got back.

When, in the middle of June, he entered Culiacán, most of his army left him. Coronado went on to Mexico City with about a hundred men, and he did not get a hero's welcome.

Above, a grass hut of the Wichita Indians.

A map of the California coast made by Domingo del Castillo, the pilot of an expedition that explored the coast in 1540-42, while Coronado's group was exploring inland. Cíbola is shown in the top center as "La Ciudad de Cibora."

THE INQUIRY

Guadalajara, New Galicia. September 1, 1544. An important and powerful judge, Lorenzo de Tejada, has been sent from Spain to hold an inquiry and pass judgment. Before him stand Francisco Vásquez de Coronado and a lawyer. Judge Tejada asks Coronado how he will answer the following charges: (1) that he had "committed great cruelties upon the natives of the land through which he passed" on the way to Quivira and back; (2) that he made war on the natives of Cíbola; (3) that he caused the rebellion of Tiguex by setting dogs on Bigotes; (4) that he had murdered the Turk.

Coronado makes a very bad defendant. He rambles, loses his temper, and can't remember things.

Judge Tejada then asks Coronado how he would answer these accusations: that, as governor of New Galicia, he took bribes, gambled, made greedy deals, played favorites, and in general was a very bad governor. Coronado's friends defend him well. But Coronado does not answer clearly and to the point. He mumbles, forgets, shouts insults, gets confused about the simplest facts.

A few years later, a court in Spain, reviewing all the evidence in the trial, finally acquitted Coronado of all the charges. But Judge Tejada and Viceroy Mendoza both told the king that Coronado was no longer fit to be governor of New Galicia. The king agreed. Mendoza allowed Coronado to keep his rather unimportant job as a city councilman of Mexico City. One of the last times anything was heard about Coronado was when he made a great fuss about who should carry a flag in a city parade.

Thus Coronado disappeared, almost without notice, from the stage of history. Spain never forgave its conquistadores for not finding gold. And Spain never forgave its explorers for not *keeping* what they had found. Coronado had drawn back from a great new land. There was nothing to show for his large, bold adventure — not even a little town or fort somewhere that might eventually become a city.

Coronado probably considered himself a failure. He had used up a great deal of his money. He had found nothing. And yet some of his own men knew what they had done. As the years passed, they realized more and more that they had been the *first* — they had gone where no white men had gone before. They had seen things that no European had ever seen before. They had suffered greatly, and they had been brave. Other men could only follow in their footsteps, and later they did — to New Mexico, to Arizona, to Texas. Perhaps if he had lived long enough, Coronado would have realized this too.

Coronado probably died on September 22, 1554. We know that only because the records of Mexico City mention that he did not show up for a council meeting as he had died a few days before. For almost four hundred years, people forgot where Coronado had been buried. Then, about forty years ago, two men were able to prove that Coronado was buried underneath the famous old Church of Santo Domingo, in Mexico City.

History has played tricks on Coronado. Some historians have said that Coronado was just another conquistador, blind with greed for gold, who killed and looted wherever he went. But if Coronado *had* been a brutal killer, leaving a trail of death and destruction behind him, history might not have forgotten him quite so easily.

Some people have praised him for discovering the Grand Canyon, which he never saw.

Some historians have said that Coronado did one thing that changed the whole history of the American West. They said he brought horses to it, horses that escaped and became wild mustangs. And so, it was said, the American Plains Indians became the marvelous proud horsemen the pioneers found — the Sioux, the Comanche, the Cheyenne. But only two of the horses in Coronado's army were mares. Only a very few new horses could have been born, and these probably would have died. The horse came to the American plains about seventy years later, when Spanish settlers went north again — following Coronado's route — and in 1610 started the town of Santa Fe, New Mexico.

More than four hundred and thirty years ago, a handsome young nobleman in golden armor rode into a strange new country. His journey took two years, and he traveled more than four thousand miles — and never found what he was looking for. The nobleman's full name was Francisco Vásquez de Coronado. Today we honor him as Francisco Coronado, or Coronado for short. But — ironically — his real name, the name he and his family used, was Francisco Vásquez.

A map of New Spain drawn
by Theodore de Bry in 1595.

A NOTE ON SOURCES

All of the major documents relating to the Coronado expedition are available in *Narratives of the Coronado Expedition, 1540–1542*, edited by George P. Hammond and Agapito Rey. Ramusio, in *Delle Navigationi e Viaggi, 1556*, refers to the report of Fray Marcos. Paul Horgan's *Conquistadors in North American History*, Herbert E. Bolton's *Coronado on the Turquoise Trail: Knight of the Pueblos and Plains*, and Paul A. Jones' *Coronado and Quivira* are other helpful sources.

THE AUTHOR

Malcolm C. Jensen is a native of Hempstead, New York. A graduate of Kenyon College and the Free University, Berlin, he has been a textbook editor and free-lance writer for ten years. Mr. Jensen lives in Los Angeles.

INDEX